Grace Reflected

Poems and Essays

Lynda Allen

Living Heartfully
2021

Grace Reflected
By Lynda Allen

Order books from: www.lyndaallen.net

Printed in the United States.

Interior photographs ©2021 Lynda Allen
Cover photograph ©jekaterina marholina/EyeEm license courtesy Adobe Stock Photos
Cover design and book layout by Lynda Allen

Allen, Lynda.
     Grace Reflected / by Lynda Allen.
     ISBN-13: 978-1-7322557-2-2

    1. Spiritual Life -- Poetry. I. Title.

Other titles by Lynda Allen

Poetry

Wild Divinity
Illumine
Rest in the Knowing

Nonfiction

The Rules of Creation

Dedicated

To those we've loved and lost so senselessly

To all the sources of grace in my life

To the fierce and healing love that you offer the world

Contents

The Alchemy of Loss

Giving Voice

How to Be in the World

Introduction

Let me begin by sharing my definition of grace. I believe that grace is love in motion, love in action. This is a definition I came to after wanting to better understand the idea of grace, but once reading about it, not finding a defintion that made sense to me. I explored the concept through my writing and meditation practices. The idea that grace is love in action felt accurate to my internal compass.

Grace then became a powerful energy in my life. To some it may seem contradictory to use the word powerful in describing grace. Yet, I believe that there is no more powerful force in the universe than love in action. Love is not a soft or weak emotion or energy. Love is a force for change, for protection, for compassion, for empathy, for labor (thank you, Valarie Kaur!), for healing. Love in motion can be raucous, consoling, fierce, beautiful, quiet, gentle, awe-inspiring, breathtaking, powerful, and so much more. All of these qualities that love embodies are also why I find the swan to be such an appropriate symbol for grace. The swan is graceful in its motion and in the curve of its neck and it radiates beauty, but the swan can also be fierce when the need arises.

Grace Reflected is just that, the many reflections of grace in my life. Sometimes grace is reflected in gentle moments spent in nature, rapt in awe at the beauty of sunlight on a tree or the curve of a wave or inspired and instructed by the flight of an eagle. Sometimes grace is reflected in the depths of sorrow, moving through grief with love and loss side by side. Sometimes grace is reflected in love's fierceness when putting love in motion through words, spiritual activism, and raising my voice in defense of, or in solidarity with, those in harm's way. Always grace has demonstrated an alchemical power to transform and heal.

I see my heart as an endless reservoir of grace and when I am in the openness of writing, the words flow through my heart, through grace, and onto the page. These words, this collection is my love in motion, my love in action. I hope that you feel touched by grace in some small way while visiting with me through these poems and essays.

Holy Moments

$\mathbf{Y}$ears ago, I set an intention to live each day, each moment from my heart. I remember so clearly what it felt like when I first set that intention. It was uncomfortable. As loving and compassionate as I would have liked to think I already was at the time, still it felt unfamiliar.

I had a frank conversation with God soon after I began this process of living with my heart wide open, with no doors to cover or shield it. I was clear in this conversation about the discomfort, and my dislike of it! I asked what happens if it falls out? Which it felt like it might do at any moment. The response I received from Spirit in that moment changed my life, or more accurately recalled me to life as I was intended to live it. The response to the question of what happens if my heart just falls out with no door to protect it was, "Good. Notice where it lands because love will grow there." I had no way to argue with that statement, and really, no desire to.

That moment was transformative and has guided me ever since. I don't succeed in living that way every moment, I am after all, a life in progress. However, since that day I have attempted to let my heart guide me in all that I do.

One of the most beautiful aspects of living from the heart is an openness to wonder and holy moments. For me, to live a full and curious life it's essential to retain a sense of wonder. The world we live in, even with all its mostly human challenges, is a miraculous and beautiful place. The astounding fact that each snowflake is unique out of the millions I see fall on a winter's day is proof enough of that. The incredible beauty of the full moon when it's light wakes me in the middle of the night is proof. The intense blue of the blue jay, and vivid scarlet of the cardinal against the snow are proof. If we pause at almost any moment in nature, we can find something to fill us with wonder and awe. In the summer I'm constantly amazed at the sheer number of shades of green! The delicacy of the butterfly's wing is a wonder! Have you ever paused to consider the unimaginable number of different types of flowers (there are at least 400,000), or species of birds (there are up to 18,000)? It truly takes my breath away. I remember one morning on a walk I stopped for a moment by a pond where a Great Blue Heron was standing at the water's edge. I was struck by the incredible array of blues and grays in its feathers. I looked around then at the flowers and trees and all the colors I was surrounded by. It was a moment when I felt so close to a Creator, by whatever name you choose to use. I felt the sheer joy that creation must be with a palette of unlimited colors! It was a holy moment for me.

I've had many holy moments in nature. I've had many holy moments in the company of humans as well. I think the ones in nature taught me to remain open to them in all aspects of my life, even at times when I might find our journey as a human race to be disappointing or challenging. If I will simply pause and be still, I allow myself the space to see the holy in a situation, I allow it to reveal itself. This is why I think it is essential that we hold on to that sense of wonder, because through it the holy can be revealed.

Reflecting now on the choice to live from my heart with wonder and awe and the transformation it brought, I wouldn't choose to live any other way. It still has challenging moments, but more than anything it is a joy. It has become more natural to me. I have to remember to do it less and am able to simply live it more. It's amazing to see the magic that happens in big and small ways when I trust the guidance of my heart. I'm so grateful that choice recalled me to life as it was intended to be lived; heart wide open and present for the holy moments.

Everywhere

There is a moment just before the veil of night falls,
drawing darkness down upon the day,
a moment when with her timid hand
she can reach out and touch eternity.
It's there, trembling in the dusk each night
for those who pause to see.

She discovered it accidentally,
thinking she was brushing aside a cobweb,
only to find her fingers disappeared momentarily into the eternal.
Everything and nothing entwined with her invisible fingers.
It's only natural, when holding the hand of the infinite,
for one's fingers to blend in with all that is,
to temporarily lose the idea of me, myself, and I.

She will tell you herself
that the first time it happened it frightened her so much
that she didn't dare look for it again for a long time,
not quite an eternity though.
Gradually, night after night
she immersed herself a little further into the eternal,
only then realizing there is no further, no distance, in eternity.
With a laugh then, she leapt,
throwing herself with abandon across the threshold of time
knowing there could be no need to find her way back
when she was already everywhere.

Winter Light

On that cusp of deep darkness
and the rising of the light,
I glimpse her through my window.
A crescent Grandmother moon
adorned with Venus,
a glowing pearl hanging below her
on a chain of stars.

I would close my eyes and return to dreams,
but her beauty draws me.
What could dreams hold more beautiful
than her light glimpsed through the starkness of
the maple in winter,
its branches outstretched
as if to catch her should she fall to Earth?

Yet she remains aloft,
drifting leisurely across the gradually brightening sky
until she is barely visible,
and her pearl completely lost to my vision.
Somehow though, having shared that moment with her,
she stays with me
and keeps me aloft
as I drift leisurely through my waking hours.

Answered Prayer

I sit beside the river and pray.
There are no words to my prayer,
there is only me in the silence, prayerful,
waiting for the words to form that can express the longing
of my soul for reunion.
The longing of my soul for the Beloved,
the one I have felt,
to appear, to take form before me.

A tail thrashes and breaks the surface of the water.
Raindrops form perfect circles as they rejoin their kin in the river.
With its prize firmly grasped in its talons following a perfect dive
below the surface,
an osprey shakes off the water like a dog.
All touch and transform the ever-flowing waters.

The Beloved recognized in each raindrop and ripple,
in each dive below the surface,
and in each stirring that reaches out from within.

Language Lesson

Why do I feel that all the answers are there on the curl of the wave?
I glimpse them fleetingly as the sun climbs above the horizon.
They rise from the water's calm surface,
up, up, toward that razor-sharp line along the edge of the wave.
I almost have them, I can almost
interpret them,
but that moment of spotting them upon the elegant curve
is gone with the break,
and they are lost among the pebbles and shells upon the beach,
seeping back into the waters from which they sprang.

Maybe the roar of the wave is the sound of the ocean's frustration
at the loss of another opportunity to share the sea's mysteries.
Over and over, she is thwarted by her own power.

Or perhaps the roar is the mysteries being spoken by the sea,
the wave her tongue, with the answers at its tip,
and it is only a language that I have yet to master.

They say the best way to learn a language is to be surrounded by it,
to be fully immersed.
I allow the mysteries to lure me into her cool embrace
and float among the waves for my first language lesson.

At Dawn

There is moment between the darkness of night
and the rising of a new day,
a moment only,
when all the mysteries of life gather together
utterly silent.

Those mysteries of the darkness
face to face with those of the light,
their secrets mingling,
reflecting each other.
The darkness passing the baton of exploration and revelation
to the light,
knowing it will receive it back again with the new day's dusk.

If you are still and silent in that moment
as darkness and light mingle,
and if you hold your head just right,
and open your eyes and heart just a little,
you can glimpse all of life's mysteries at once
and see the baton pass.

You might be able to convince yourself that it was only a dream,
but for that new thought or unimaginable wonder
that slipped from their grasp
into your waiting heart
as night passed to day.

Piercing

An unknown bird sings.
Other sounds are dampened by the fog
yet its song pierces the veil.

That is how I feel about God
a voice, a wisdom, a presence
that can pierce the veil
of my human fog
and let the song of the Divine
wash over me.

*O*ne night my lovely husband Bill came to me and said, "You have to come outside." As he took me by the hand, I thought to myself that the moon must be full, and he wanted to show it to me. On my way out the door a firefly landed on my hand to offer me a clue.

May is an amazing time of year in our yard. There are so many fireflies that it looks like December with all the trees lit up with twinkling lights! As I stood there in the dark, I was filled with wonder and delight watching the lights floating all over the yard. When I feel filled with awe at the beauty of nature, laughter often bubbles up from the sheer joy I feel. That night was one of those moments.

Living from the heart, present in the moment allows for that joy to bubble up and express, because it allows us to witness the wonder that already exists all around us. It allows us to set aside the norms of how we "should" act, and simply express the joy of being alive. If you've ever been in the presence of the Dalai Lama, you can feel that joy emanating from him. We only saw him from a distance at a speaking engagement and yet we could still feel it. He has much to distract him from joy given the circumstances of his people and all the traveling he does, and yet he is able to maintain that sense of joy, his face often lighting up with laughter like a child! Too often we don't allow ourselves the freedom children feel to laugh out loud with glee.

Yes, the world can be filled with things that are indeed serious and we must be present with them as well. But we can't allow the serious to prevent us from being present for the joyful and wonder-filled moments. I lost a dear friend in the spring of 2019. For me, being present with the grief I was feeling was equally important to being present with the joy of that light-filled field on a dark night. After all, isn't it those moments of being fully present with life and with those we love, that helps create a life that gives cause for mourning? I believe that to be true. So, I will continue to mourn, but I will also continue to stand in wonder and joy and allow the laughter to bubble up.

A Map Home

I.
"You have to come outside," he says.
A firefly lands on my hand on the way out the door.
Over and over, it calls out,
using nothing but light.

When I reach the darkness of the yard, it takes flight
and looking up, I see that they dance all around me.
They are a little earlier than usual this year.
It is mid-May, but it looks like December,
the trees aglow with twinkling lights.

I can understand the temptation to capture them in a jar
and create a living lantern,
but to truly take them from the sky, from their dance of light,
seems a crime too grievous.
Who am I to steal the light from the night for my own pleasure?

I am content, delighted even,
to simply witness their flight,
to try to trace one light as it blinks off here only to glow again there,
writing their secret messages across the dark night sky.
Perhaps if I stand here long enough,
I will begin to be able to decipher their Morse Code –
one long glow, then two short.
Better yet, I will lay in the cool grass
and let the mystery of illumination fill my vision
and my being.

II.

One firefly followed me to my room,
after I reluctantly left them to their dance.
I wonder for a moment if it was the same one
who guided me out into the night.
I watched with joy his blinking message crawling up my window.
I tried, but sleep would not come
and when I again opened my eyes,
there he was, on and off with his light beside my bed.

"A firefly found its way in," I whisper with a smile
to his sleeping form.
I laugh quietly as it takes flight around the room,
blown off course occasionally, as if battling a gale,
by the breeze from the ceiling fan spinning its endless circles,
a flightless propeller.
Does the firefly taunt him with flight,
or bring him the gift of witnessing it?

To my eyes his flight seems erratic, and yet,
if only I could trace his course
perhaps, I would discover written
the answers to all the questions of the Universe,
or maybe a map leading me home.
Then again, maybe I do understand his message
as I lie with joy radiating from me,
bright enough to illuminate any darkness.

Alive

A catbird calls, melodic and sweet on the morning air.
How do you explain the value of his song,
of simply being present in the vastness of the universe
in this moment to hear this particular song?
It is an occurrence never to be repeated in all of time.
It is a song that I may be the only human to hear.
One tender, precious instance of life pouring forth in melody.

Of course, no value can be assigned to being awake in this moment,
to hearing my heart echo the catbird's sweet song,
to the elation of being vibrantly, achingly alive on a spring morning.

Awakened

Prior to last night, I didn't know beauty could awaken me.

She woke me with a firm yet gentle touch,
a fingertip of moonlight brushing my eye lids.
Groggy, I reluctantly opened my eyes to discover what culprit
had disturbed my dreams,
only to find moonlight draped across my pillow
like the long, silver hair of a lover.
I followed the path of light it had laid out for me
and caught my breath when I saw that the cedars
were not just illuminated by its glow,
but rather were robed in it, like King and Queen of the Night.
Only now do I see why the tops of the trees are called crowns.

The fox, not one to be left out,
added his voice to the beauty of the night,
calling first from a distance,
then from directly below my window.
A traveling bard performing for Their Majesties,
spinning tales of night's mysteries.

How can one shut out such beauties and return to slumber?
I will never know. I chose to remain awakened to beauty.

If you have never perused Maria Popova's Brain Pickings website, I would highly recommend it. In her own words, it is her "one-woman labor of love exploring what it means to live a decent, substantive, rewarding life." There is such a wealth of beautiful writing there, though I will warn you, it's easy to go down the rabbit hole by following links within the articles!

As I let her weekly newsletter lead me down that rabbit hole on one occasion, it was just one line in a letter written by William Blake that caught my eye; "As a man is, so he sees." Seven simple words that express something so profound. One of Blake's examples in the letter is this; "The tree which moves some to tears of joy is in the eyes of others only a green thing which stands in the way." We could all look at the same object or person and each see it differently. How you see the world says a great deal about you. It's not good or bad, but it does say something about you and what you value in life.

Which brings me to a question, one that I've asked myself. If you had to make a list of the five things that were the most important to you in life, what would make that list? If you find that five is too few, start with ten. Then try to narrow it down to five, then three, then just one thing. It's an interesting exercise that encourages you to look at what you truly value most.

Then consider if you saw the world and everything and everyone in it through that lens of what is most important to you. Knowing what you value most, when you looked again at Blake's tree, what would you see?

For me, it is a valuable process that can help me shift how I'm looking at a situation, object, or person. I only need to remind myself to return to seeing through the lens of what is most important to me. Of course, remembering to remind myself can be part of the challenge! But once I do, I can see things so differently. As I am, so I see. Thank you for the reminder, William Blake, and Maria Popova.

Packing for the Journey

What if the past is a backpack that I put on each day,
and each morning when I rise,
I choose what I will carry forward with me?
What if I imagine that each memory, each moment of my past
weighed the same, traumas and celebrations alike?

If today is a journey I am about to embark upon,
what do I pack?

I look to the journey of this day and sort through what I have laid out.
I pack memories that will keep me warm.
I pack the map of lessons learned to help me find the best route
  forward.
I pack the knowing of those in my life who will walk beside me.
I pack the wisdom of my ancestors, and my love for those I've lost.
I pack my circle of friends, like a life preserver I always have if
  needed.
I pack moments of joy and laughter as a reminder that sorrow has
  a companion.
I pack insights gained to use as a cushion for moments of quiet
  reflection.
I pack the love I have received, as a gift I know I can now give to
  others along the way.

Pausing, I find that my bag is nearly full.
If I really wanted to, I could squeeze in hurt feelings,
or that grudge I've been carrying.
However, there certainly doesn't seem to be room
for that person I've been choosing not to forgive,
or that disagreement that I didn't want to let go of.
Well, maybe I could squeeze that one in!
Or, better yet, I could leave a little space in my pack for growth
and begin the journey of today a little lighter than the day before,
not weighed down by the past.

Schooled by Peace

Peace takes various forms.
Today its form is elusive.
I cannot find it in the usual places -
upon the cushion, among the trees,
between the words.

Does the seeking of a thing cause it to become farther out of reach?
Must I walk toward peace as I would a frightened animal,
slowly, cautiously, with soothing tones?

Shall I cast a line out for it, with just the right bait,
so that I can then draw it nearer to me?
If I am quiet enough, will I hear the words of peace whispering
and let them flow as ink through my waiting pen?

Today, it seems, peace came calling subtly, through questions.
Asking me to set aside all I thought I knew of it until now
and to simply allow myself to be the form it takes on today.

Cacophony

The air is filled with sound.
Far above me, a small plane putters along,
but nearer to me, the jays call insistently back and forth,
the cardinals chirp and peep,
birds uncountable speak in tongues I can't translate.

Above me, on a branch dripping with the maple's red buds,
a grackle expresses its displeasure at my presence
in squawks and screeches,
though, perhaps, it's the cat's presence he protests
rather than my own.

A call I've never heard before reaches me among the others.
So great is the din on this spring morn,
that I cannot isolate it from the rest to memorize its song.

No method to mute all the other sounds and hear just the one song,
as I so often I long to do;
simply let the noise fall away
and hear just the one voice singing.

Call to Contemplation

A bell chimes in the distance.
There is a church nearby.
It is their Sunday morning call to contemplation.
I pause and listen to the call.
It draws me within, not to be confined by the walls of a church,
but to the cathedral within,
the place of prayer and stillness that is my own.
It is a space created solely for me,
a personal, holy space for reflection, respite, and guidance.
I'm not the only one carrying this sacred treasure.
It comes with the equipment.
There is no assembly required.
An assembly of one is enough.

December Morn

I watch the blue jays chase each other around the branches of the
  cherry.
Occasionally, they pause in their pursuit to search a limb for
  breakfast.
Their sharp cries perfectly describe the crisp coldness of the
  December morn.

In the distance the hawk calls, looking for its mate,
their voices always clearer this time of year.
If the hawk drifts nearer
the jays will let me know.
Their chatter of breakfast found, and playful games of tag,
will turn to an alarm reverberating through the treetops,
"Beware! Beware!"

Each day a birth.
New life coming forth from the dark comfort of night's womb,
a tentative breath,
a small cry,
as the new day emerges.
All the possibilities of an unlimited future
that a parent could hope for,
seen in the waxing smile of the setting moon.

And the jays cry,
"Be aware! Be aware!"

Holy Union

There is a moment of holy union
just before the sun rises,
just before the day fully wakes,
just before the spark of life ignites.
In the stillness between the exhale
and the birth of the new breath

there is a moment
of holy union.
It is a moment of mystery,
and creation,
a moment of the undefinable taking on form,
the old mingling with the yet to be,
reaching out for each other in the stillness,
and finding between them
the holy.

Arising, from the holy union
found in their embrace,
my daily rebirth.

ɞɜ3ભ

The Nature of Things

When beloved poet Mary Oliver passed away in January of 2019, she took with her a light that illuminated the beauty of nature, an eloquence to describe the human condition, and insights into the spirit. Luckily, she left behind much beauty of her own. I'm without words to adequately express how sad I felt knowing that her words had stopped flowing here on Earth, though I treasure each one she gifted to us before she took her leave.

There was such a sense of mindfulness to her poems. I don't think she could have captured the moments she did in nature without having been fully present in those moments. That's one of the things I love about her work, that feeling of presence and her way of expressing the joy found in being present. She was so aware of the moment that she was able to capture it in words that draw me into the experience with her, as if we are standing there together, as if the words had moved through my own heart, just as she hoped for in her poem "I Want to Write Something So Simply." Her poems confirmed for me that nature is one of my greatest teachers, if only I will be still and present within its embrace. It is there that I always find grace reflected.

One thing I have in common with Mary Oliver is a love of swans. I had a beautiful experience when I was reading her poem "Swans" in *Evidence*. As I read it, specifically the moment when she ponders where the swans go, all I could think was, "They come here, Mary. I welcome them here after they leave you." It seemed a strange thought, but I could just picture her watching them take flight, leaving her there on the ground in New England and me taking up the watch, as I awaited their arrival here in Virginia. A connection across the distance through grace on the wing.

After her passing, I went to visit with the swans and read them her poem, letting her words float through the cold winter air to reach them across the surface of the creek. They were silent until it was time for me to leave, when they raised their voices, trumpeting their thanks and mine to Mary.

Swans

Still comfortable in my bed, my heart called me to the park.
My intention was to walk in the woods,
a few moments of peace among my friends the trees.

Instead, I wandered down the hill toward the lake
and found its surface aglow with swans.
"The swans are here!"
The words sprang from my lips unbidden,
as if they had been there since waking waiting to be spoken.
Always the words seem to know something I do not.

I hurried to the shore to be nearer to them –
my joy as bright as their feathers.
The surface of the lake was perfectly still,
not wanting to disturb the reflection of their beauty.
My feet led me to the dam, which created the lake,
so that grace had a place to land.

The geese nearby began to squawk and took flight.
A boat approached, quietly but steadily.
The swans too began to raise their voices.
I looked with distain upon the one who would disturb such a moment.

My distain forgotten as grace took flight.
The swans lifted off as one.
Their melodious voices rising with their wings,
a clapping sound as the tips of feathers slapped the water's surface.

My eyes and heart both wide with awe and wonder,
they flew straight for me,
a wave of grace washing over me.

29

I watched as overhead they split elegantly into two groups,
like dancers in perfect unison releasing
only to reunite on the next beat,
all the while composing an unforgettable performance of light,
voice, and movement.

The low-lying clouds able only to swallow their form,
but not their song,
they reemerged; the clouds pulled back as for a curtain call.
My vision was filled with their flight.
Low they came overhead calling,
"The swans are here!"

My joy overflowed, wet upon my cheeks,
as I watched them back into the cloud's embrace.

Nudes

I much prefer spring and summer
with their color, warmth, and light.
Yet, as I look to the trees at the edge of the field
I feel an unexpected sorrow knowing that soon
much of their form will be hidden,
clothed once again in green.

Only now do I see them as graceful nudes
hung across the gallery of the sky.
I have been walking among the pathways of the world's greatest
art museum,
seen the artist's finest masterpieces,
and until this moment had not learned to appreciate
the technique and style of his brushstrokes.

As if my newly awakened eyes cause the models to become
self-conscious and modest,
I can almost see them reaching for their verdant robes.
Voyeur or not, I will enjoy their naked forms a while longer,
before they are brushed once again by spring.

Red Fox

I shared a moment with a red fox on a cold January morning.

My breath made small clouds of mist
as I stepped quietly outside at the sight of him.
I had intended to shoo him away
  for fear of his intentions toward our cats.
Instead, I paused,
  as did he, at the sound of the door.

We both simply looked at each other,
held the other's eyes from twenty feet away.
It seemed like no distance at all in that moment.

It felt as though a season passed,
and we ran, and played, and tumbled,
and hunted together at dusk and into the evening.

That moment when our eyes met
  I knew what it was to be a red fox.
I wonder if he in return knew
  what it meant to be a human being.

If he had to learn it from me
  his lesson was incomplete,
  as I am always still learning,
  still exploring what it is to be human,
while I'm certain that he knew what it is to be a fox.

As he trotted away, after a moment or a season,
pausing twice to look back over his shoulder at me,
I knew in some unexplainable but certain way
that we both walked away with a gift that morning.

Daffodils

It's February, and the daffodils have started to push up
through the earth.
The eagles are more active above Mother River.
While many places are blanketed still in snow,
here, Mother Earth sends small signs of spring.

The daffodils always know.
Something within them sends the signal to grow
at the first return of warmth,
but when the conditions change
they slow their growth, even pause.

It's Nature's game of red light, green light.
When Winter turns her back,
the wily daffodils rush forth
reaching toward Grandfather Sun.
When Winter again turns her eye their way,
they freeze in place,
hoping she didn't detect their motion.
Finally, when our journey around Grandfather Sun
chases Winter away for another year,
the daffodils run gleefully forward to touch the sun,
blooms in hand.

The Calm

We are in that moment that fills me with anticipation and delight
each year.
You will miss it if you're not paying attention.
It is the calm before the spring.

Winter's long train is all that remains of her here,
though I can see her back in the distance,
as she journeys on to her next destination.
If she glances over her shoulder, there may yet be another frost.
All keeps still and calm so as not to attract her attention,
like a rabbit hoping to escape the eye of the hawk.

If she continues on without pausing, the storm of spring will break.
Colors will gather in the morning sky like rain clouds
and colors will burst from the ground
forming puddles of flowering green mosses, and deep purple crocuses.
The daffodils with their yellow hoods drawn, will throw them
back and raise their joyful faces to the warming sun.
Songbirds will gather in flocks and sing a song of farewell
to Winter as she recedes.
Frogs, countless frogs, will wriggle their way out of damp, dark,
muddy places
raising a ruckus each night,
proclaiming the reawakening of the slumbering earth.

Summer's End

The black walnut's leaves have begun to change and fall.
Just a few for now,
  enough to signal a shift though.

Like the flock of geese cutting the air with their arrow tip
above the river the other day.
I have seen them around all summer raising their young.
There was something different this time,
something about their numbers and orderly formation
that wasn't there before,
an intent,
a leave-taking,
a farewell.

My heart feels that sinking feeling it always does this time of year.
Summer's end weighs heavy,
whether with the weight of the coming snow,
or of the passing years, I'm not certain.

Perhaps it's merely a remnant of childhood days
spent carelessly in the sun, splashing in lakes,
climbing out with a layer of brown on our skin from the cedars.
The summer that seemed never-ending,
coming to an end.

If only I had the grace of the black walnut,
and could face loss with such ease
and practiced release.

The leaves have begun to change
and fall.

Whispers of Growth

The leaves are all gone from the maple.

The sweet cherry lost hers much earlier,
she's not as healthy as she once was,
yet, there are those last few, clinging to a high branch
nearest the warmth of the house.

Though it appears stark,
and I can feel the cold of the approaching winter
through the thin panes of glass,
still the branches in their barrenness,
hold within them the promise of spring.

Even when the gusts of deepest winter sweep through,
tugging at those last few leaves,
I will be able to hear among the branches the whispers of growth
that linger in the wind's wake.

So, I remain still,
embracing the cold, without letting it in,
holding the memory of light and warmth within,
following the lead of the learned maple, and sweet cherry.

Grace Reflected

I feel the glow before I see it.

As I approach the water's edge,
my breath hanging in the air in puffs of palest gray,
I see with some part of myself that I cannot name.
I know she is there, gliding upon the water,
my heart rejoicing before my eyes can confirm it for the mind,
and drink her in.

Finally, the trees lift their branches from my eyes and reveal her.
The water a smooth, black glass reflects a perfect copy of her.
She appears lit from within, so bright is she upon that dark surface.
That's how it is sometimes,
only with the contrast of the darkness can you truly see
the beauty of the light.

She turns her head my way and pauses.
Slowly the ripples cease, and her small wake settles,
until there is only stillness.
Her perfect expression of grace
doubled in the dark mirror of the water.

◦❧ 4 ❧◦

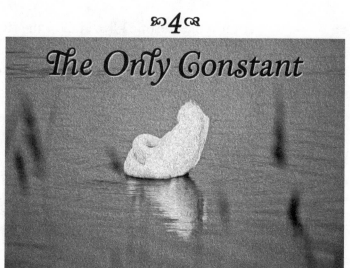

The Only Constant

*I*t's funny in a river town like the one I live in, how the river touches all our lives. During a recent spring when the river (Mother River to me) was particularly high, it seemed that everyone in town was out on a Sunday evening wandering around in awe of the power of the flooding Rappahannock. We often use the word raging when we see the river so full and moving so swiftly, but that makes her seem angry. To me she just needs to rise up every now and then and stretch and express her power. It's a good reminder that we are part of nature, not in control of it. Watching huge trees bobbing along on her surface like insignificant toothpicks was enough to demonstrate that.

Of course, it's a good reminder in another way too. There are times when our life seems to be overflowing, with joy, sadness, grief, work, stress, celebration, challenges. It's important to remember to try not to judge and label those moments, like when we say Mother River is "raging." In that same spring, my life seemed to be overflowing with changes. Within two months of each other, my older daughter graduated from college and my younger from high school. Those were big changes for all of us. What kept flowing through my mind was David Bowie's song "Changes." There's a lot of wisdom in that song, but the line that I kept coming back to was the one that talks about turning to face the changes. Face the changes. Yet, change is something we tend to avoid. We prefer instead to look away, or think we can control the changes, just like we think we can control nature. Until the flood.

It's those moments of flood when we can learn the most, if only we will turn and face whatever that flood is. I think the key is what we face the flood with. We must begin with awareness, just as the youth in Bowie's song are aware of what they're going through. If we face whatever the flood is with awareness rather than resistance, we can live through the flood of what we're going through with more grace. We have a better chance of learning the lesson, healing the wound, making the connection, etc. with more gentleness. If the flood is too much stress, we can turn and face it with stillness. If it is grief, we can

40

turn and face it with compassion for ourselves. If it is joy, we can turn and face it with presence, so that we can fully appreciate and absorb those moments of joy.

As I moved through the flood of changes that time brought to my daughters' lives and to my own life, I attempted to face the flood with awareness, presence, and with patience with myself. I wanted to be present in each moment with them. I strove to be patient with myself as the tears flowed in unexpected situations, like while simply making breakfast with them one morning. I wanted to be immersed in the joy of celebration as they graduated and planned for their next steps. And most importantly, I had to connect with the stillness within myself, so I could be present with them as they faced their fears about the unknowns before them.

For me it's the difference between being pulled under by the flood and floating along on the currents like those trees. The thing to remember about floods, is that despite the tearing down and scouring that can happen, they also leave behind much that is fertile, allowing opportunities for rich new growth.

Lesson from a Juvenile

A juvenile eagle flew over as soon as I arrived.
As I neared the parking area, I stopped to watch a young deer;
a buck with only the first tips of antlers showing.
He was all alone. I watched for several minutes and no others
were nearby.
A baby all alone was what my eyes and heart saw.
How does nature always know the lesson I most need to learn?

She left for college today.
I park my car, not really sure why, and walk to the picnic area.
I had thought it was about time to head home,
but that still small voice led me here instead.
I have the space to myself, and as I sit alone on the bench
say aloud, "I don't know why I'm here."
I enjoy being on my own with the birds, so I simply look out on
Pope's Creek and ponder my own question.

As I let my eyes wander across the expanse of the creek I see them.
An eagle and osprey engaged in a chase,
almost as if they knew that was what would catch my attention.
"Well, the point isn't that far. Maybe I'll wander over,
since I'm here."

Even from a fair distance I hear the calling,
over and over, urgent, and high-pitched.
There is an osprey nest with at least four ospreys nearby,
one protesting at my approach.
I pause a while wishing I could interpret
the advice she's giving her young.
Is it the same advice all moms give when a threat nears?

When I arrive at last at the point, I see eagles across the water.
One breaks off as soon as I arrive and heads my way.
As it nears, I can see it's a juvenile.
It makes straight for me, soaring over my head, as I smile up at it.
Strong, capable, breathtaking, sure of its flight.
No interpreter needed.

Preflight

I feel unbearably vulnerable,
as delicate as the casing that surrounds me.
I want only to remain curled tightly,
safe within my walls.

At some immeasurable point, just before birth,
protection becomes prison.

As safe as I feel here within this shell,
there is a deep call to break free.
As I grew, the walls did offer shelter,
yet, I mustn't remain behind them too long,
lest my safe haven becomes my spirit's tomb.

I was created to fly,
but what bird can fly with its shell still upon its back?

The walls tremble now
with each new breath.
The light rises as the walls continue to thin,
if I could but glimpse it,
make one tiny crack to peek through.

I uncurl just enough to reach uncertainly
toward the light.
A shudder, unbidden, runs through me as I brush the wall,
now the source of my confinement.

There is the briefest moment of choice.
A slight pressure.
To my surprise it takes only the smallest pin prick in the wall
to flood my cell with illumination.

The urge to fly overcomes all fear,
and I stretch and push,
no longer hesitant.
The walls, having served their purpose,
fall easily away,
and I stumble blindly into the light –
nothing so graceful as bursting forth!

As the last shards of my shell settle around me,
I stand unsteady in the cool air of the new day,
knowing I'm not yet ready for flight,
yet knowing I am ready for the steps
that strengthen my wings
preflight.

Protection becomes prison,
becomes platform
for flight.

Lazarus

The maple seeds are falling like rain,
twirling, twirling to the ground all around her.
Maybe that's what did it,
or maybe it was the song that awakened the memories.
The notes and words slipping through tiny cracks beside the stone
that had been rolled in place to block that tomb.
She had listened to it often during that time,
it helped her release
and heal.

She hadn't suspected it would catch her unawares one day
and reawaken the feelings, like Lazarus rising from the dead.
Where she thought she had healed, had laid it to rest,
still, there lingered pain.
Not like it had been, and not with a desire to raise something
long since dead,
but the memory of the feeling of loss like a bottomless chasm
in her heart.

Tears flow freely as the tiny helicopters continue to twirl and land,
with much more joy than her tears do,
yet with similar purpose,
a release that creates growth.
And so, she allows the stone to be rolled aside, the tomb to open wide,
and the dead to walk free.

I have learned so many powerful lessons sitting beside the Rappahannock River, and have processed innumerable issues and changes in my life while sitting on her banks and being present with what's happening around me. Life itself is an amazing teacher. I'm deeply grateful for the insights I've gained by being still and watching it unfold. Mother River has been one of my most effective mindfulness and life teachers! Mindfulness, after all, isn't all about being still with your eyes closed, it's about being still and present, wherever you find yourself in that moment.

As I was having lunch by the river one spring day, I saw a small green leaf drifting under the water. As I watched, I noticed the leaf seemed to be moving strangely, so I looked more closely. Then the leaf swam toward the bank and crawled up on a rock! It was an adorable, tiny, baby turtle! I couldn't help but sit there letting the joy bubble up inside me. I then watched as this tiny turtle would alternate between resting on a rock and then throwing himself back into the water and battling against the flow of the river. Sometimes he would make it a little way upstream and sometimes be pushed back. I watched him do this over and over.

I had my own internal struggle as I sat watching him. Should I help him? I wanted so much to pick him up and move him to safety, but would that truly make him safe? If I moved him, maybe a predator would catch him more easily. If I moved him, maybe he would lose his way. It also occurred to me that maybe that struggle is what he needed to do to help make his little legs stronger. I realized that all I could do was to sit there on the rocks and cheer him on with joy and love and wish him well on his journey.

Eventually, the river took him further downstream out of sight. It was a wonderful lesson though. As much as we might want to pick someone (including ourselves) up and move them out of a situation or struggle, maybe it is what they need to make them stronger. Maybe that's the moment when we learn how to guide ourselves and we won't learn it if someone else picks us up and puts us where they think we should be. It's an excellent reminder from a parenting perspective as well. So, I returned to the stillness and sat by the river trusting that the turtle's instincts would guide it well, and let it go on its way with love and with the knowing that someone witnessed and held the space for its struggle. Maybe there are times when having a witness is enough.

My Love

There's nothing to fix, my love.
I am not broken,
>though I feel that way sometimes.

Though I feel that way sometimes,
>I am not broken.

There's no path to find, my love.
I am not lost,
>though I feel that way sometimes.

Though I feel that way sometimes,
>I am not lost.

There is no one here to rescue, my love.
I am not drowning,
>though I feel that way sometimes.

Though I feel that way sometimes,
>I am not drowning.

Though I am whole,
>still there are cracks that let light in.
Though I am arrived,
>still the winding path led me here.
Though I am buoyant,
>moments below the surface of darkness taught me to value
>light and life.

I am not broken.
I am not lost.
I am not drowning.

Yet, in my love I am whole enough to feel broken.
Yet, in my love I am found enough to feel lost.
Yet, in my love I am buoyant enough to sink.

There is no place for you here, my fear.
I am love,
   though I don't feel that way sometimes.

Though I don't feel that way sometimes,
   I am love.

Four Words

"I never feel beautiful,"
said so quietly, so vulnerably, I almost missed it.

Four words.
Four words from a beautiful woman, who doesn't see her own beauty.
Four words that make me want to weep,
that enrage me,
that break my heart for every girl who's ever thought them.
Four words that echo back to me my own self-doubt.
Four words that stop me in my tracks,
and leave me standing, looking in the face of a woman
beautiful in every way,
without four words to offer in response
that will help her see for herself what I see.

After all, what power can words have over every image she's ever seen
of airbrushed, Photoshopped beauty,
every image of unattainable perfection,
attained only through clever lighting, makeup, scalpels,
or just the right body cinching undergarments?
What words can I offer to erase each one she has spoken to herself?
If I hadn't spoken those very same four words myself,
then maybe I would know what to say
in the face of such beauty and such doubt.

I don't have the words to heal the wounds,
but I do have two eyes, and a heart that see her clearly.
Yet, my heart doesn't call me to respond with
trite words of reassurance,
but to say instead, "When you were born, beauty took form as you."

51

Your beauty deepens with each smile.
Your beauty deepens with each kindness,
with each loving word,
with each gentle touch,
with each gift of your time,
with each sharing of grief or laughter.
With each expression of love, another layer of beauty settles upon
you like morning dew upon the flower.

You needn't concern yourself with feeling beautiful, my friend.
Beauty rejoices as you.

Four words.

The Alchemy of Loss

*H*ave you ever had the experience of your heart trying to tell you something? Mine was trying to tell me something a few years ago as I began to type "a peace filled morning to you!" which is my usual greeting for my weekly inspirational email. Only on that morning, I typed "mooring" instead of morning. Something told me to listen to what my heart had to say.

When I stopped to reflect on it, I realized I had actually been thinking a lot about moorings; things that keep us secured in place.

There are times when those lines that keep us secured to something can be beneficial, and there are times when they feel like they are holding us back. Knowing the difference can be tricky. Finding time for silent reflection on a regular basis helps me see the differences clearly.

I had been thinking about the subject at that time for two reasons. Both were challenging situations. One situation in which it came up for me, was in relation to grief and loss. Of course, being moored somewhere is not a permanent condition. We can always weigh anchor and move on, and I guess that's a way of describing our transition out of this human life. We simply move on to another port. But what do we do when someone we love is no longer moored beside us, has let go of their Earthly tether? It can certainly make us feel adrift too. It seems to me that at those times it can be beneficial to lengthen the connection that holds us in place, give it a little slack so we can extend a little farther than we have before, yet remain connected to that place where we feel grounded. It's not productive to fight against the tide of grief. Sometimes we need to be able to just be in the drift of it for a while, and surrender to its currents, all the while knowing that connection back to safety is still there.

That connection back to safety remains. That's the other perspective on the idea of moorings that I had been looking at. The son of a friend was in a serious car accident. She had been sharing the journey of his recovery through social media. What struck me so profoundly about witnessing their journey from afar, was the tether they provided for their son as he recovered. The doctors had to keep him under sedation much of the time due to intubation and multiple surgeries. All the while his family was there beside him, taking turns spending the night at the hospital with him, talking to him, holding his hand. In moments of consciousness, he made attempts to communicate, and he was slowly healing. It was, and still is, a long road to recovery. Every step of the way though, they were there to let him feel that tether, that connection to them and to their love. It felt like someone who is floundering in the water, but has been thrown a lifeline, and that line was their love. Gradually, when he was able, he pulled himself to the surface using that line and caught his breath, basking in their love. I have no doubt their love will remain a source of life for him as he continues his recovery.

It seems there is a question we can ask to help us determine whether a mooring line is holding us back or is something that offers safety and support; is the connection one that is woven from love? I think it would apply to many things; relationships, a job, where you live. Is your connection to that person or place one that is based in love? If so, it can help us weather those times of discomfort, challenge, or transformation. If not, it may be time to raise that anchor and move on.

That brings me back to grief. We don't get to make the choice regarding when a loved one moves on from this life, and too many times I have found myself grieving for someone who has moved on long before I think they should have. Maybe all my writing about moorings was simply to give me a new way to look at loss. It gave me comfort after the loss of a friend. I could visualize her connection to Earth and to the hearts of those who love her as just being a lot lengthier. We had to let that tether slide gently through our fingers and give her enough line to go as far as she needed to. While she's no longer moored here in place beside us, we can still reach out and feel that connection woven with love whenever we need to.

Alchemy of Loss

What a weight this human heart.

Normally a mere ten ounces or so,
today it is heavy with loss.
How is it that the weight of memories increases
when we have lost the one the memory holds?
Does the gravitational pull on the memories somehow multiply
as our loved one breaks free of that same gravity,
so that what once was light and joyful,
now weighs heavy upon the heart?
For it was those same moments in the living of them
that made my heart light,
which I now feel the full weight of.

How does that transformation occur?
Joy transformed so easily to sorrow through the alchemy of loss.

The heart must hold the secret that alchemy is a long process though,
for somewhere it knows that one day the gravity will again reverse,
as the weight of grief upon my chest lifts,
and I can delight once more in moments shared,
with the same joy in which they were created.

The leaden weight of grief transformed
into the gold of treasured memories of love.

Who Will Speak the Blessing?

Heads are bowed,
eyes are closed,
yet no voice is raised.
Who will speak the blessing?

Without agreeing to,
we left a space in the circle.
One day, we know the circle will close, and we will fill the space,
but for now, who will speak the blessing?

Today, we simply let the silence be -
the echo of our loss,
reverberating in the space left behind.
No one speaks the blessing.

Hands instinctively reach one for the other,
hearts join in a moment of shared grief and grace,
transforming the silence.
Love speaks the blessing.

Grow the Good

A box arrived in the mail.
A small rectangle the size of a video tape.
Remember those?
Folded neatly inside was a t-shirt,
soft and sky blue,
with the words "Grow the Good" surrounded by butterflies
and "Peace and Wonder" below, on the pages of a book.

As soon as I saw the box and the return address
I knew there would be so much more than just the t-shirt
folded up inside.
A gift from a friend who would give you the shirt off her back
and did just that,
before she moved on.

The tears flowed as soon as I unfolded it,
felt the soft fabric and held it to my cheek.
I wept for myself,
which I sometimes forget to do.

What I didn't know, was how the unfolding would continue.

As I sit now, days later, I can hear the chainsaw buzzing.
I know it's cutting through the limbs of the sour cherry tree
beside the house.
I went out to say my goodbyes before it began,
on this quiet, cold, winter day.

As I looked at her bark, so covered in lichen
and the branches that would bear no more fruit,
I could feel the need for letting go when it is time.

I could understand when someone is tired and ready to move on.
They've spent their life energy, are weary of the fight to survive,
know they have done their work and are ready to let go.
I knew the difficulty of being the one saying goodbye.
The pain that there are no words for
as you move between understanding the need to let go
and the reality of letting go.
There is a chasm there,
which no amount of tears or words of love can fill.
It simply has to be a chasm,
empty and wide.

So, I stood with my heart against the cherry tree
tears spilling onto her trunk
and whispered, "I love you"
and let the ache be there
and let the tears flow
and let the anger rise alongside the guilt.
Then I looked up among her branches
and offered thanks for the beauty,
the shade, the tart nourishment,
the greenery and cascades of pink flowers each spring,
the perch for my bird friends.
I spoke my gratitude for all she had given me with joy in my heart,
while at the same time lamenting
how different the view from my window will be,
how big the hole in the sky will be,
how empty I will feel.

Standing at the chasm,
so like that small box,
wondering how much it can hold -
my heart, my grief, my love, my loss, my lessons to learn,
my gratitude, my joy, my unfolding.

A t-shirt now a treasure.
A piece of wood now a canvas.
I place them each gently within my heart
knowing how much it can hold,
and move forward with the seeds they each planted there
to grow the good.

The Stages of Grief

They say there are stages of grief,
as if in our grieving we are actors in a play.
If only there truly were a script to work from,
so that when we reach the end of Act III
the curtain falls and we exit, stage right, with our grief left behind
upon the boards.

Instead, we stumble from one stage to the next
blinded temporarily each time by the glaring spotlights
that illuminate each.
There are no cheers or standing ovations for our performances
as functioning human being,
as grieving friend, as heartbroken widow or widower,
as inconsolable parent.
There is only the absolute silence after the lights have dimmed,
and the crowds have gone home.
The deafening, echoing silence of a voice we won't hear again,
a laugh we would trade anything in the world
to hear fill the house once more.

What does the actor do when done with the stage?
How do they leave the play behind, set aside the words
and move on to the next show?

I find I remain frozen upon the stage, lights dimmed, seats empty,
words fallen silent, at a loss for anything to say that can heal or revive.
I do the only thing left to me.
I sit on the edge of the stage, feet dangling, swinging.
My feet, at least, free of the stage.
So, I let them swing, reveling in the feeling
of even a small part of me being free,
and ignoring the twinge of guilt that sense of freedom brings.

Suddenly a spotlight springs to life,
illuminating a circle of light behind me.
There, within a crisp, clear, perfectly-formed circle of light stands
my grief.
My cry of anguish the moment I heard the news, each tear that
I shed, each truth I denied, each shout aimed at the sky and
at you, each fear I wouldn't utter or face, each moment of aching
loneliness, each moment of complete confusion about what to do
next and how to go on, even each thought of not going on,
but also each joyful memory of love and laughter shared,
all gathered together in that beam of light.

My loss taken form at the end of an unscripted Act IV.
No soliloquy, no accolades, no stellar reviews.
Just my grief revealed in the light.
Revealing also, grief has a life of its own.

Finally, I leave the stage.

Icy Heart of Winter

The wise text speaks of stillness, of being bare, being stripped to
  your essence,
    like the winter trees.
What it does not say is how to live with that feeling of nakedness.
How to be still and release as the winds strip each leaf away.
How to reconcile grief with the truth of change.
How to feel radiant in your raw essence,
  rather than exposed and alone.
How to find beauty in emptiness.
How to remember that you will again someday both create
and receive nourishment
  with the return of the sun's light and warmth.
How to allow the aching loneliness to be, without pushing it away,
  without trying to fill it with noise.
How to remember that you are still rooted, still strong,
  just resting before the next cycle of growth.
How to thaw the icy heart of winter.

The Tulip

The black cherry is in bloom,
and the lilac.
Oh, the lilac! So sweet I can taste its scent!

My friend lost her husband last week.
Unexpected and sudden,
like that tulip beside the river.
One day, as I walked along, the view was just different.
The splash of scarlet among the grasses that had caught my eye,
suddenly gone.

I had expected to watch it go through its whole cycle of life,
expected to continue to enjoy its beauty each day,
and gradually bear witness to each petal as it faded and fell away,
like red snowflakes melting in the spring sun.

Instead, a hand reached down when I wasn't looking and picked it,
took it to enjoy on their own,
but robbed the rest of us
of all but the memory of its beauty and grace.

The Blade of Loss

Loss, sudden, unexpected, sharp
tries to cut out the place where you resided,
but you are deeply rooted, where even loss's blade can't reach.

I turn toward yesterday,
and wonder what I was doing at the exact moment you left.
How can it be that I was feeling joy at that moment?
Shouldn't the world have grown silent and reverent?
Or even raucous? You would have liked that better, I think.
At the very least, there should have been a bell tolling in the distance.

There will be times ahead when I will wish I had loss's precision
with a blade and could remove my grief with a few swift strokes.

It is not to be so simple though.
The duel between grief and I will be ongoing.
In the end I will prevail,
my love for you my shield, deflecting the blows.

For now, I will allow the pain and tears to flow
through the wound left by loss's first stroke,
and wonder if somehow that was its intended purpose.
A hit so well-landed, a blade so precise?

I first shared the poem "Packing for the Journey" in July 2019. One week later it took on new meaning when there was an accident on the four-lane road near our home. We couldn't get home because the road was closed due to the severity of the accident and the medevac helicopter on the roadway. Around 6:45 pm we parked our cars across the highway at a church and walked home. Only one lane of the road was open again by 10:30 pm when we went to get our cars.

There was a fatality in the crash. It was a young man driving on his own for only the second time. The friend that was with him also died days later in the hospital due to his injuries. That's why the poem took on more urgent meaning for me. We hope that only good, or at least manageable things will happen during the course of our days, but life is obviously unpredictable, a truth that the year 2020 made abundantly clear. So, truly, if this were my last day, what would I bring with me into the day? It may seem an overly simplified answer, but in light of the events of that night the answer really is this simple: I would pack only love. I don't think in that moment of leaving this life I would be thinking of the things that frustrated me, or the things I had accomplished, or even the things on my bucket list (if I had one!) left undone. I would be thinking about those I love. Not about politics or whether I was right or wrong about something, but about how much I had loved and how much I wanted to live so I could continue to love.

Maybe we can continue to love on even beyond this life. I believe we can. No one can offer proof of that though, so why not love now, in this moment? And if you do believe in a life beyond this one, what if all you have to recommend you, all you have to take with you into the next life to create from, the only currency you're allowed, is the love that you gave while here? It's an interesting thought. What if the love we offer here in this life is put into a kind of savings account on the other side? How full would that account be when you arrive? If love is as important for survival in the next life as money is here in this human one, how well will you be able to live there based on what you paid into it while here? It's a thought-provoking question for me.

The question I asked myself on the night of the crash was, "What can I do?" It was a hot July night, so, we brought water bottles to the rescue workers. It seemed a small thing. It didn't seem enough, so in the end, I went outside before the light was gone and made the only offering of love I could for the young man who lost his life, a prayer, and some words on paper.

Route 17

Someone died on the road near our house today.
I don't know who it was.
The road was closed, and we couldn't get through to get home.
The medevac's blades were still whirring nearby,
settled on the road like a gigantic dragonfly.

I parked my car at a church and walked home.
I can pick it up later,
a small inconvenience,
and I'm not that big a fan of cars at the moment anyway.

I got out a red wagon and filled it with bottles of water,
walked slowly down the street, wagon in tow.
It was 95 degrees and Virginia humid.
I looked away from the car covered by a tarp.
The rescue workers were not able to look away.
The tarp was green.
A shiny, black, unmarked van arrived. I didn't want to know why.
We set the crate of water for them by the side of the road
and left with our wagon.
What else could we do?

I worried that it was a new driver,
unsure of the rules and right-of-way.
I worried that it was a family, or an elderly person, or someone I knew.
All the what ifs cascaded through my mind.
What if it had been someone I loved?
What if I hadn't stopped at the store on the way home?
Someone else's what if became a reality this steamy summer evening,
with one ring of the phone.

It's strangely quiet outside, as I sit and offer a prayer –
still air, no traffic noise,
only crickets, a cardinal,
someone cutting the grass as if nothing is wrong.
What else can they do?

Maybe the crickets' song is one of mourning.
Maybe the cardinal's song is helping guide someone home.
I sit quietly, letting the what ifs float off with the emerging fireflies,
or at least trying to.
All I know for sure, is that tonight I will have ice cream
and savor each bite.
What else can I do?

Pearls

With your departure from this life, you are reduced to memories
and photos.
As if your smile or laugh could truly be contained in those.
How you always did manage to smile through the challenges
I'll never know.

What makes a life then?
Is it how you live?
Is it what you leave behind?
Is it how much you loved?

A life isn't a grand sweeping epic.
A life is moments,
one by one strung out like pearls on a strand of time.

Moments spent.
If a moment were currency, how would you spend it?
That is what makes a life,
how you spend the precious currency of your moments.

Once they are spent, they are irretrievable,
you can't earn more of them or save them up for a rainy day.
We each get a lifetimes' supply, and no more.

Some get more than others,
yet in the end it is not the number of moments you string together
upon the thread of a lifetime,
but the quality of those moments —
the softness of them,
the kindness you created them with,
the love contained in them, both given and received,

the friendship offered within them,
the music and harmony they echo with,
the lessons you were aware enough to learn,
the laughter they were brightened by,
the tears that watered them,
the gratitude they were lived with,
the grief they were shattered by,
the silence they were held with,
the sacredness found within them.

String them together with care.

A Good Meal

Life is more than what you eat,
yet it is like a good meal.

Life is who you choose to break bread with.
Life is the quality of the ingredients you select, and the care
  with which you select them.
Life is where you choose to dine.
Life is how you prepare the meal, with love and intention,
  or haphazardly.
Life is how quickly you eat, savoring each bite or
  devouring it without really tasting the flavors.
Life is whether or not you begin with gratitude.
Life is how long you linger over each course.
Life is the laughter and conversation during the meal.
Life is saying yes to dessert, often.
Life is contentment when the feast is done.
Life is parting with an embrace, and well-wishes for a safe journey
  until we meet again.

Everyday Things

Picking up this pen to write.
Awakening to sunlight and birdsong.
The softness of the cat in your lap and the sharpness of the claw
in your thigh as she settles in.
The warmth of a worn pair of slippers and the comfort of a worn
pair of jeans.
The happiness that floods you at the sound of a friend's laugh.
Cool water on your skin as you dive in.
Feeling the gentleness and intimacy of fingers interlaced.
The sound the refrigerator door makes when it opens.
Inhaling the scent of breakfast cooking on a Saturday morning.
The feeling of returning home at the end of a journey.
Brushing your teeth.
Thunder rolling across the sky.
That contented fullness after a good meal.
Watching your favorite movie, for the hundredth time.
Taking a deep, lung-filling breath.
That endorphin high after exercise.
Communing with the trees on a morning walk.
Turning on the lights as the day fades.
Settling in with a book as the rain falls upon the roof.
Sipping a hot drink on a frigid day, or a cold drink on a sweltering day.
The laughter of children.
The sound of toast popping up when it's ready.
Just the right pair of sunglasses for a sunny day.
That shade of red that you only see once a year when the maple
leaves turn.
A hug that continues to hold you long after you part.
The silence that accompanies a snowfall.

Everyday things.
Precious, taken for granted, everyday things
that shine like stars in a night sky,
distant and unreachable,
yet, breathtakingly beautiful
when seen from the distance of loss.

Well Lived

Let me not come to die with a pristine heart,
a heart with nary a scratch or crack,
a heart devoid of the signs of a life of love.

Let me not come to the end of my days
with a heart that doesn't bear a small scar or two,
healed over, yes, but with the marks of love and empathy upon it.

Let me not come to stand upon Death's threshold,
ready to journey joyfully across,
without knowing the resilience of a heart that has been stretched
beyond its capacity,
by both love and sorrow, for they are traveling companions.

Let me not take my last breath without knowing
the boundless nature of my heart,
its ability to give without measure,
and yet, remain full.

Let me not come to gently shed this human life,
freeing my soul once more,
without a grateful bow to a human heart,
that was able to remain open,
whose door was thrown wide to embrace life with love,
to allow love to expand,
to be a safe space for others to be seen,
to rest,
and to heal.

Let me not come to lay down this life
without knowing gratitude and joy
for a heart well lived.

ఴ**6**ఴ

Giving Voice

I had the opportunity to go on a social justice trip through the James Farmer Multicultural Center at the University of Mary Washington before the pandemic kept us from doing such things. We traveled by bus to retrace a portion of the path of the Freedom Rides. That weekend I was immersed in stark reminders of the extremes societies go through and was reminded that we need to consider how we might be contributing to those extremes and choose our actions accordingly. Which side of history do we want to find ourselves standing on? Where would love stand?

As I walked past display after display of the immense courage of regular, everyday people I was moved to tears. As I walked past display after display of the immense hatred of regular, everyday people I was moved to tears. I thought about the people in the photos looking back at them now; pictures filled with images of dignity, fear, courage, rage, hatred, violence. How would they feel looking at those photos now if they were the ones displaying the hatred, inflicting the violence, acting from rage? Would they wish they had made different choices then, given what they know now? I hope so. I hope that if they could go back in time, they would choose love, understanding, and the courage to face and explore differences rather than fear them.

Over and over again throughout the trip we were faced with the courage of the Freedom Riders. They prepared themselves for the violence they would face as best they could through role-playing. How prepared can you be though, for hatred so clearly and violently displayed? Where does that kind of courage come from? Not only did they get off the buses despite the presence of angry mobs, but after they were brutally beaten and patched up at the hospital, they got back on those buses to go to the next town. They got back on those buses. Tears arise when thinking of the courage that took.

At the beginning of the Rides, there were thirteen Freedom Riders. Thirteen people with courage I can only imagine, who set out to create change through nonviolent action. That choice and the violence they faced, eventually inspired hundreds of others to ride.

People came from all over the country, from all walks of life, students, adults, and elders alike to ride the buses and get jailed in Mississippi. They sang freedom songs and filled the jails. These were average people with above average courage who took action because they wanted to create change, because they wanted to be on the right side of history, the side that stood for love and compassion and equality.

Where would love stand? Where would love have me stand today? During a year as tumultuous and focused on social justice on so many levels of society as 2020, I found myself asking that question again and again. Where would love have me stand today? I marched. I wrote letters. I raised my voice. I supported organizations fighting for social justice. I voted. Even with all that, the most important things I did were listen and learn. I spent a lot of time educating myself about issues I found I knew very little about, like the prison industrial complex. I spent a lot of time reflecting on the benefits my privileges in life have offered me. It was and still is uncomfortable and essential work. I don't think I can make a stand with love without having listened first to those whose voices I am trying to help raise, to help amplify. I don't think I can make a stand with love about issues that I don't know enough about. It's my responsibility to listen and learn and then use my presence, my voice, my financial resources, my privilege, my vote to help find solutions that make a more equitable society.

So, I began by looking at where I was standing with and for love and where I wasn't and tried to choose accordingly. I asked myself, where am I in relation to the extremes we are seeing? Where am I contributing to them either knowingly or unknowingly? Then, made choices accordingly. I reflected on my own biases and am working to shift my thinking and internal programming and act accordingly. I consciously wear my "Changing the World by Changing Me" t-shirt from singer Jonathan Santos, and start by changing my own heart, by opening my own heart, by finding the courage there to love beyond any fear and stand for love everywhere I am.

The most profound way I have found to stand for love and to work for change is to allow the change to happen to me through the words that move through me. When faced with the overwhelming emotions brought up by the courage of the Freedom Riders, the tragic loss of lives to mass shootings, the hate crimes, and police violence toward people of color, the hundreds of thousands of lives lost to the coronavirus pandemic, or any of the suffering I see every day in the news, I find myself processing through words.

The journey of writing is transformative for me. I'm constantly amazed by the path to healing it helps me find that I could not see from where I began, especially because so often the only starting point I can find is just to be present with the anger, rage, fear, grief, or sorrow. From there all I can do is allow the words to carry me and guide me to a place where the healing can begin. From that place I can see more clearly where love would stand and choose my actions accordingly.

*The subject matter of the poems in this chapter may present triggers for those who have gone through traumatic experiences or who are sensitive to violence or the suffering of others. Please honor yourself as you need to by skipping over them or reading them when you are ready. Whenever you are ready, please consider reading them with someone who loves and supports you.

Forty-nine

"The funerals have begun."
Forty-nine of them, when all is said, and done.
Forty-nine of them, so far.
Forty-nine of them, this time.
Forty-nine eulogies.
Forty-nine days filled with the mourning of hundreds of hearts.

As a nation we offer our thoughts and prayers.
How many prayers exactly, are equivalent to a life?
How many thoughts to assuage the loss?
How many empty words falling from the empty mouths and minds
of politicians and pundits, does it take to fill the void?
Whose voice will be raised at each funeral for those
who no longer have a voice?
Who will speak forty-nine times for the fallen?
Who will stand up forty-nine times, or weep forty-nine times,
or rage, or grieve, or sing songs of praise,
or scream, "Enough!" forty-nine times?

Who will forgive forty-nine times?
Jesus said to forgive seventy times seven times.
Shall we wait then,
until the body count reaches 490 rather than 49?

And whom shall I forgive?
The man with the gun in his hand,
or the one who sold it to him?
The man with hate in his heart,
or the one who taught it to him?
The man filled with self-loathing,
or the ones who should have loved him?

The man with a vengeful God as his inspiration,
or the one who preached to him?
The one blinded by rage,
or the ones who blinded him?

How do I even begin to forgive the unforgivable?

The larger question perhaps,
who and what do I become if I don't,
if I can't,
if I won't?
Without forgiveness I become filled with hate, and fear,
and self-loathing, and vengeance, and rage.
Without forgiveness, I become number fifty.

For the 49 people* killed at the Pulse nightclub on June 12, 2016
in Orlando, Florida.

*Names listed at the end of the collection.

A Child Walking Home

He had the face of a child.
On the cusp of manhood, yet still with that hint of a baby face.
Life laid out before him, filled with possibility, challenge, triumph,
failure, love, sorrow, all life's glories.
His sweet, child-like face though, was wrapped in black skin.

His skin somehow blinded the other to the child,
to the future walking there, candy in hand.
Instead, he saw only enemy, only danger,
where no danger existed.

All that existed there before him was a child walking home.
A child whose mother had to warn him about situations like these
as she raised him,
because she knew only too well about the blindness,
how the color of his skin would blind others to his true nature,
to his humanity.
They would see only the color,
not the child she loved,
not the man he would become,
only the man they feared he would become.

Now, none of us will see the man he would have been,
for in his blindness, the other followed, confronted, and with intent,
killed him,
then stood by while all the possibility, challenge, triumph, failure,
love, and all of life's glories drained out of him onto the pavement.
All except sorrow,
sorrow lingered in that child-like face a while,

and left a stain on that street which remained
long after his spirit left,
long after his mother came for him.

For Trayvon Martin, killed at the age of 17 on February 26, 2012
in Sanford, Florida.

I Will Not Be Quiet

I will not be quiet.
I will keep shouting,
"They are all our daughters."
Every one.
Each girl that is raped on a college campus in Virginia,
or on a bus in India,
or as an act of war in Africa,
or in her home by a relative,
or by a professional athlete,
or by a teacher,
or by a celebrity.
Every one of them,
they are all our daughters.

Shaking our heads and being angry will not suffice.

I will not be quiet.
My voice will be raised in opposition.
My voice will be raised for safety.
My voice will be raised for justice.
My voice will be raised for respect.
My voice will be raised for education.
My voice will be raised for solidarity.
My voice will be raised for peace.
But make no mistake,
my voice will be raised.

I will not be quiet to protect your reputation.
I will not be quiet to protect your good name.
I will not be quiet while you sweep it under the rug.
I will not be quiet while you look the other way.

When you look the other way, you will find me standing there.
When you pick up your broom, I will take away the rug.
When you speak your good name, I will speak truth.
When you look to your reputation, I will hold up a mirror.

I will not be quiet.
Our daughters deserve better.
And they are all our daughters.

For too many to name.*

*More information at the end of the collection

What Was Lost?

I don't even cry anymore.
How many people died in that nightclub in California two weeks ago?
I don't even remember.
What were their names?
I didn't look for them.
I didn't look for their names.
I didn't read their stories.
I couldn't.
I couldn't feel it again.
I couldn't cry again.
I couldn't be outraged again.

And so they died, and I didn't feel it.
And so part of me died, and I didn't feel it.

I'm numb.
Does that mean they have won?
Whoever they are.

If someone wins,
what was lost?

I would tell you that a mother lost a child,
but we don't feel that anymore.
I would tell you a husband lost a wife,
but we don't feel that anymore.
I would tell you a person lost their best friend,
but we don't feel that anymore.
I would tell you a child lost their father,
but we don't feel that anymore.

I would tell you a country lost its way,
but we don't feel that anymore.

For the 12 people* killed at the Borderline Bar and Grill
on November 7, 2018 in Thousand Oaks, California.

*Names listed at the end of the collection.

00:00:01

Watch the footage from a security camera at Dragon Wok
in Minneapolis, Minnesota
on May 25, 2020,
but pause at 20:36:48.

It's not the video of the moment a police officer
places his knee on George Floyd's neck
while he is handcuffed and face down
on the pavement.

It's not the moment when George Floyd,
with the knee still pressed into his neck,
cries out that he can't breathe,
but gets no relief.

It's not the moment when witnesses
are calling out again and again
saying that George Floyd is bleeding
and can't breathe.

It's not the moment when other police officers
try to keep the passersby
from watching what's happening,
when you can clearly see the knee is still pressing
into George Floyd's
ever more lifeless body.

It's not the moment when the officer finally removes his knee
from George Floyd's unconscious body
and he is rolled, limp,
onto a cloth stretcher,

91

the last glimpse the world,
including his loved ones,
get to see of him
presumably alive.

It's none of those moments.
It's a moment I shouldn't have to share,
because we should already know
his humanness.

It's a moment when George Floyd,
with his hands cuffed behind his back,
is sitting on the ground
his back against the wall
his knees pulled up
clearly in distress
his head falls to his left knee
he shakes his head in frustration or disbelief,
we will never know which,
he taps his head against his left knee two times
and shakes it again.
It's a gesture so familiar,
so human.
You recognize it. I did.
That moment of asking,
"How did this happen?"
The resignation,
the defeat,
the despair.

We won't ever know what George Floyd was really thinking
in that moment.
He died

under some man's knee
    with people all around,
        only some of whom
            could see he was human
                and cared that he was dying.

What do you see at hour 20, minute 36, second 48?
Why do we need to look through the footage
the high school and family photos
talk to the friends
see the crying children
search the work history
to find the human being?
Why isn't it just there in his face
walking by on the street,
well before the head hung in despair
and the knee taking his last breath?

Why isn't it just there in his face
at hour 0, minute 0, second 1
at his first breath?

For George Floyd killed by a police officer on May 25, 2020
in Minneapolis, Minnesota.

Souvenirs

There's a postcard of a lynching.
It was a regular practice.
It wasn't unusual to have a photographer present
at a brutal murder.
Someone to document the torture,
the dismemberment,
the remains.
Not to document it as a crime,
but rather as you would
any important,
memorable event in your life.
A souvenir you could buy
to remember
a murder by.

It didn't matter
that it was someone's husband,
son,
brother,
or mother.
It didn't matter whether or not
they committed the crime
of which they were accused.
There was no trial, no defense
for being black-skinned
and alive.

They gathered, rabid and eager,
and let every fear, every base human instinct,
every ignorant thought
have reign.

They surrounded,
yelled, pushed, jeered,
hit with fists or sticks,
kicked,
burned,
hanged,
and cut fingers and toes -
postcards weren't the only souvenirs.

With each action, a click, and a step.
The camera's click capturing
each step
further
and further
from our humanity.
Click. Step.
Click. Step.
Click. Step.
Never once pausing to focus on the fear,
the pain, the stark inevitability
in their prey's eyes.
After all, he wasn't actually human
to them.

Click. Step.
Click. Step.
The sound carries
(can you hear the march of the Third Reich approaching?)
through the humid, southern air,
through the stench of charred remains,
through the smoke,
all the way to the darkroom
where the pictures are developed.
All the way to the printing press

where the postcards are manufactured.
The thriving business
of souvenirs.

Click. Step.
Click. Step.
Until the sound of change in a pocket
is added
as a souvenir of murder is sold,
and carried home
to preserve the memory of a time
another's life
was stripped of dignity, humanity,
breath.
A memory of a time
when we all took one step further.
Click. Step. Ching.

And the sound carries further
than they could have imagined
to a quiet southern evening a century later
when a young man
in a red hoodie
accused of no crimes,
but walking and breathing,
and having black skin,
is followed, confronted, and killed
and instead of postcards
paper targets are sold
featuring a silhouette of a young man
in a hoodie.
Click. Step. Ching.

And the sound carries further
than they could have imagined
to an evening in Minneapolis
when a grown man
is pushed to the ground
with hands cuffed behind his back,
his pleas for help ignored,
as a knee presses,
and presses,
and presses
on his neck
as effective as any noose,
while, as at any lynching,
the assailant's comrades stand by,
watch, and do nothing.

No more click,
just the silent press of a finger
on glass
to record eight minutes and forty-six seconds
of murder.
Ad revenue goes up
for news outlets who run it,
selling murder and
anxiety medicine
is big business.
Press. Step. Ching.

If you look closely at the footage
you can see the shadow of the rope
from not so long ago
that created the noose
for Trayvon and George
and so many others.
Souvenirs of the past

that keep bleeding
into the present.

Without a different kind of change
found in hearts rather than pockets
the only remains
will be souvenirs
of what was once
our humanity.

For the thousands* lynched in the United States, in both the past and the
present.

*More information at the end of the collection.

There have been many times in recent years, and throughout 2020 in particular, when I found it a challenge to remain peaceful and loving, especially when I read or listened to the news or scrolled through social media. With all the debate and division that has been a theme in the United States and around the world, the idea of spiritual activism - engaging, healing, awakening, seeing another's suffering, and working for change from love – has been a topic of importance to me. How do I engage in conversations about the challenges we face and remain peaceful? What is the most effective way to create change? Where do you even begin to create change? How do I contribute to the healing we need? How do I work for change and equality with love? I admit that I have been feeling deeply challenged to live from and with love throughout 2020 in the face of such hatred and in the face of the choices people made that were so harmful and dangerous to others. I've had moments of thinking spiritual activism is all well and good in theory, but does it apply when thousands, even millions, of people are suffering? What can love can do in the face of pandemics, hatred, racism, political division, and so much more?

Each time I face one of these questions, I come back to the same knowing. At my core, I genuinely believe that love is the most powerful force for change, the most powerful inspiration to live the best version of ourselves. There is nothing else I would rather face pandemics, hatred, racism, and political division with than love. Returning to love is what has always gotten me through my darkest moments. Why would it not get us collectively through our darkest moments as well?

Writing is what I turn to when I am facing difficult questions or when I can't seem to remember how to return to love. On November 8, 2016, the date of the presidential election between Hillary Clinton and Donald Trump I wrote the poem "Love Outside the Lines." It was a hopeful poem in a moment when I needed a little hope. In 2018, when I wasn't sure how to love those I disagreed with so vehemently, the words of "Before" flowed forth to help me return to love. Returning to love serves both me and all those with whom I interact.

I believe spiritual activism is at its most powerful and effective when I am actively doing the inner work that returns me to love, that heals my own wounds, and awakens me to the truth of others. Then I can bring that more awake, more healed, more loving self to the conversation about change in our society and in our world. I can speak more effectively about change when I am speaking from a place of peace and wholeness within myself. I can work more effectively for change when I am able to practice not taking anything personally. I will help create more lasting change when I can look at the "enemy" or the "other" through the lens of love and see their suffering. Being still within myself allows me to engage rather than enrage. We are both more likely to hear each other that way, and when you get right down to it that's what people want; to be heard.

It's important to remember that the work of spiritual activism is not about having to agree with each other, and it doesn't mean condoning or overlooking harmful actions taken by others out of fear or hatred. It means that we engage with the fierceness, strength, and wisdom of love to create a better world where none doubt their own worth or their own contribution to the whole, and where all feel safe and know they are loved. I believe we create this world by beginning with our own hearts, by creating from the love within ourselves and sharing it unconditionally. It is not easy work, but the reward is a more loving, more compassionate world.

Before

Before all of this.
Before all the anger and fear, disharmony and divisiveness,
name-calling and judgment.
Before all of this,
you were just you
and I was just me,
tiny sparks of life -
living.

Before all of this.

I must remember you before I met you,
before I heard of you or read your Tweet.
I must remember you before I knew you,
before any labels of other, different, or enemy could be applied -
and stick.

I must remember you before all of this,
when you were new to the world,
simply love in expression.

Before all of this.

If I can remember you then,
before all of this,
then I can love you before we meet.
If I can love you before we meet,
then I can find common ground, work peacefully for change,
discuss rather than argue,
heal and forgive,
and love on,
after all of this.

So, for my sake and yours,
and for all those yet to come,
I will go back
and love you
before all of this.
So that when we do meet,
and maybe disagree,
I will already know how to love you,
through all of this.

Motivate the Base

Motivate the base.
That's the term they use
again, and again.
They are skilled at it.
They do it with precision.
They do it with intention.
And the intention is just that
to motivate
the base
instinct.

They call out to that animal instinct,
the primeval
in each of us.
They call out not to Lincoln's
better angels,
but to our own fallen ones.
They prey upon our fears
like vultures circling,
scenting their next meal.

If they want us to vote,
they prey upon our fears about our bank accounts,
or unborn babies.
If they want us to hate,
they prey upon our fears about "the other"
taking our jobs, our neighborhoods, "our women."
If they want us to follow blindly,
they prey upon our fear of hell
and invoke an unholy God.

They are predators
who prey upon
the base.
We will no longer be their prey.
We will call upon our better angels
and stand in their light
together.
We will refuse to become prey
to our fears.

Lost Between the Stars and the Earth

I.

I'm lost between the stars and the earth.
My words are like the star, whose light has traveled immeasurable distances to reach me,
a burning point of light whose source may or may not still exist
when its light is finally perceived by my eye.
These words have reached you, after traveling an unknowable distance,
a burning point of light whose source may or may not still exist
when these words are perceived by your heart.
Still, we each shine,
for it's what we do, in our different ways,
not because we hope we will reach another,
but because we have light.

II.

I'm lost between the stars and the earth.
Lost between the wonder of the vastness of space,
the beauty of galaxies,
and the vastness of the distance between hearts,
the ugliness of our words and deeds.

I'm lost in the harsh words we throw like darts.
We draw a bullseye around "the other,"
and throw words like "them," and "those people,"
pointed and sharp,
without pausing to witness the impact
when they hit their mark.

They say that space is silent.
How presumptuous to say the stars have no song,
the galaxies no voice.
Let not the space between us be silent.
Let us find common songs,
and hear each other's voices.

III.

The eagle soars overhead,
closer to heaven than I dare fly.
Maybe from that great height our small lights appear
as distant stars, warm and bright.
If only I could witness from the height of the eagle,
and not get lost in the distance.

Yet, here I am,
lost between the stars and the earth.
Will you meet me in the distance?
It's nearer than you think.

Negative Space

There is a space between us.
It is artificial,
   it's not really there,
yet it appears real when you look at it a certain way,
just like that image of two vases,
   or is it two faces?
Or is it both?

That's the trick,
   what we see in the space between us.

That space can hold all that we fear -
separation, loneliness, our differences, violence, darkness, loss -
until that is all we can see or feel.
The fragile vase of all our fears.
Fear creates the negative space.

What if we were to shut it all out -
the noise, the clamor, the propaganda, and preconceived notions -
and let our focus shift, and leaned into the space and looked anew?
Maybe all we would see was a face,
   a perfect reflection of me in you.

You and I create the positive space.

Love Outside the Lines

While love is often jubilantly colorful,
as far as I know it's not limited to one color,
not red
or blue.
I will color outside the lines that have been drawn around love
and scribble my way to you.
Lines on paper, check marks in boxes cannot limit my love.
I will love you tomorrow as I did today,
even though I know it's sometimes challenging
to love outside the lines.
I hope you will offer the same to me.
And don't forget that when we allow our colors to blend,
we create something new.

Many Lights

I want to write about trees,
and that hawk that flew so low over my car yesterday
that I felt I could reach up and touch it.

I want to bring those things with me into my day.
Instead, there are headlines that horrify me,
spelling out suffering that lingers in my thoughts
and follows me,
like a shadow which no amount of light can dissipate.

That's the fear that accompanies me throughout my day,
that there isn't a light strong enough to create a world without shadow.
Then I remember that, truly, one light can't eliminate shadow.
Only when you have many lights shining on an object
from all directions
can you overcome the shadow.

Today, I will reach up for the hawk,
walk silently among the trees,
and shine brightly.

The Miraculous

The miraculous eludes me.

I cannot walk upon water or calm the seas.
I cannot transform water into wine or make the blind to see.
I cannot multiply the fishes and the loaves or live eternally.
I cannot.

Or can I?

I may not be able to walk upon water,
but I can walk across the ocean that divides us, a hand outstretched.
I may not be able to calm the stormy seas,
but I can calm the turmoil within myself before I speak or act.
I may not be able to transform water into wine,
but I can transform hate into love, anger into peace.
I may not be able to make the blind to see,
but I can open my own eyes to those in need and reach out.
I may not be able to multiply the fishes and the loaves,
but I can take what I have and break bread with you.
I may not be able to live eternally,
but I can live fully present now, offering my heart to all.

Maybe miracles are simply tiny moments of truth,
of seeing beyond what appears on the surface.
Maybe miracles only require seeing the potential that lies hidden
in the water,
or seeing the wholeness through the seeming brokenness,
seeing the Divine in your perceived enemy,
seeing the communion that could be shared in a loaf of bread
and a fish,
seeing life eternal in the connection between my heart and yours.

The miraculous through me.

How to Be in the World

I sometimes struggle with the meanness I see in the world, on the road, on the news, on bumper stickers, on social media, in our leaders. It can become overwhelming. It can make me feel like there is more unkindness than kindness. It can make me feel that I don't know how to be in the world right now. As I was noticing how it was making me feel, as I was lamenting and wondering why people can't just be nicer, I heard a little voice within me. It said, "Why wait for someone else to be kind? Why not be the one who offers the kindness?"

It was an eye-opener. It's not that I was going around being unkind. Instead, it was a question of if I want to see more kindness in the world, why not create more now, myself? What would I lose if I kindly let that person over in traffic, yes, even if they didn't use their turn signal? What would I lose if I let that person behind me in line at the grocery store go ahead of me because they only have two items? In the end, the real question was what would I gain? I would gain a smile from a stranger. I would gain a peaceful feeling within myself. I would gain a world where a person feels good about another human being, where a person feels touched by kindness. I would gain exactly the kind of world I was lamenting didn't exist anymore.

For me that begs the question, what if the only thing needed to make the world a kinder, more loving place is my own choice to make a more conscious effort to be kind? What if I'm the tipping point we have all been waiting for? What if you are? If I knew that I was, I wouldn't hesitate to make that choice. So today, I will choose as if I am the tipping point and will start making a kinder world by being present with kindness each moment. I know I will at times forget, but I believe in the power of intention. Today, I make a kinder, more loving world.

I will begin with you. I offer a Metta or Loving Kindness practice for you today:

May you be happy.

May you be peaceful.

May you be safe from harm.

May you have oneness of heart, mind, body, and spirit.

How to Be in the World

The question repeats again and again,
with each news report, or political crisis,
or atrocity of man against man.
How to be in the world?
How to be in the world
when the world is in turmoil,
when what I thought was true, or real, or solid isn't?
How to be in the world
when the world no longer feels welcoming or kind
or never did?
How to be in the world?

I look to the eagle for how to be in the world.
I watch his purposeful flight, not a flap of the wing wasted,
sometimes gliding, letting the wind do the work.
Using his keen eyes to watch from a heavenly perspective,
then with swift, decisive action he dives,
taking from the earth only what he needs to live.

I look to the snake for how to be in the world.
I observe the stillness he achieves in the midst of his surroundings.
I note his ability to know when the time has come
to shed and leave behind that which he no longer needs.

I look to the trees for how to be in the world.
I see them bend and sway with the howling winds and raging storms,
standing tall again after they have each inevitably passed.
I see them reaching always for the light,
drinking it in and transforming it into nourishment and life.

I look to the sunflowers for how to be in the world.
I note how they keep their faces always to the light,
constantly aware of where it is in relation to themselves.
I see how their whole life is spent in creating seeds
that will bring new life after they are gone.

I look to the river for how to be in the world.
I see her always flowing with what comes her way,
sometimes reaching well beyond her boundaries,
and sometimes falling low,
yet always moving forward.

I look to a baby for how to be in the world.
Wide-eyed with wonder, learning each moment,
knowing instinctively that life depends upon
relationship with those around us,
never questioning that a cry for help is natural.

It's natural, how to be in the world.

Gravity

How do you measure and quantify a word?
Shall I scoop them up with a tablespoon,
just the right amount of love and sorrow to fold together
for a happy life?
Maybe I can count them,
the number of hurtful ones vs. the number of those kindly spoken
totaled up neatly on a spreadsheet.
Or I can line them up in a long row,
end to end,
and measure the distance they have carried me.

Still, none of these methods ring true.
I think then, I will consider instead the weight of a word.
Do I carry it around upon my back,
like a mule with its daily burden?
Or is it light like a feather,
that when combined with others serves to lift me
so that I may soar?
Does it sit heavily in my heart
like too large a Thanksgiving feast in my stomach?
Or does it burst wide my heart,
like a child's soap bubble,
with expansive joy and wonder?

Where is the scale to place each word upon,
joy,
love,
hate,
regret,
forgiveness,
so I will know the consequence of their weight

before I speak them, or before I pick them up to carry with me?
Perhaps, if they were labeled by their weight,
we could choose to let the heaviest fall away,
allowing their gravity to remove them from our vocabulary.

Sacred Text

From your first breath to your last,
each blink of your eyes,
each word spoken, whispered, or shouted
each action taken
each kindness offered, or withheld
each choice made
each moment of love, or moment of hate
each thought
each hug and each kiss
part of the sacred text of your life.

What if upon your last breath
that book is complete
and placed in the library of Time
for others to read?
If you knew each insignificant thing you did was sacred,
was written with care in delicate script,
in an eternal tome meant to guide others,
would you write your story differently?
Would you pause now and then to consider the scribe
capturing each moment?

Each second is a new letter.
Every moment is the birth of a new word.
Thoughts develop into sentences,
actions into paragraphs.

Your life speaks volumes.

Magic

Do I believe in magic?

I do, because one morning the wind blew through my window when I called.

I do, because when I thought of flying, the eagle came to share his joy of flight with me and I laughed with delight.

I do, because I knew before it happened that the snake beside the path would come say hello, and he did, coming straight for me and placing his head upon my boot before departing down the trail.

I do, because as I walked among the trees admiring their crowns, a voice within said, you can't only look up, you might miss something, so I stopped and looked down and there, where my next step would have been, was an enormous, Buddha-like toad looking up at me.

I do, because each snowflake out of millions is unique; and there are hundreds of thousands of different flowers, and colors, and birds, and trees; and the sunrise is different each morning; and each type of bird has a different song; and rocks have stories to share if only we will listen; and babies are born remembering God, the memory is there in their eyes; and ants can carry many times their own weight; and a single note of music can move you to tears; and bumble bees with such small wings and such large bodies can fly and help create life and nourishment among the flowers; and hummingbirds joust; and cats can see in the dark; and owls can fly without a sound; and a child's laughter can lift anyone's spirits; and hearts can connect across miles and across the divide of life and death; and the river can be my teacher if I am still and pay attention; and a star's light travels over millions of miles and still shines brightly enough to illuminate and inspire; and this giant ball we live on spins and offers life through air and water; and I can breathe and my heart can pump, sustaining life, without me thinking about it; and I am aware of my own existence and tiny place in a vast universe filled with things not yet seen, but still imagined.

Do I believe in magic?
If I'm awake, how could I not?

Notes

The names of those killed at the Pulse Nightclub in
Orlando, Florida on June 12, 2016

Akyra Monet Murray
Alejandro Barrios Martinez
Amanda Alvear
Angel L. Candelario-Padro
Anthony Luis Laureanodisla
Antonio Davon Brown
Brenda Lee Marquez McCool
Christopher Andrew Leinonen
Christopher Joseph Sanfeliz
Cory James Connell
Darryl Roman Burt II
Deonka Deidra Drayton
Eddie Jamoldroy Justice
Edward Sotomayor Jr.
Enrique L. Rios Jr.
Eric Ivan Ortiz-Rivera
Frank Hernandez
Franky Jimmy Dejesus Velazquez
Geraldo A. Ortiz-Jimenez
Gilberto Ramon Silva Menendez
Jason Benjamin Josaphat
Javier Jorge-Reyes
Jean C. Nieves Rodriguez
Jean Carlos Mendez Perez
Jerald Arthur Wright
Joel Rayon Paniagua
Jonathan Antonio Camuy Vega
Juan Chevez-Martinez
Juan P. Rivera Velazquez
Juan Ramon Guerrero

Kimberly Morris
Leroy Valentin Fernandez
Luis Daniel Conde
Luis Daniel Wilson-Leon
Luis Omar Ocasio-Capo
Luis S. Vielma
Martin Benitez Torres
Mercedez Marisol Flores
Miguel Angel Honorato
Oscar A Aracena-Montero
Paul Terrell Henry
Peter O. Gonzalez-Cruz
Rodolfo Ayala-Ayala
Shane Evan Tomlinson
Simon Adrian Carrillo Fernandez
Stanley Almodovar III
Tevin Eugene Crosby
Xavier Emmanuel Serrano Rosado
Yilmary Rodriguez Solivan

The names of those killed in at the Borderline Bar and Grill in Thousand Oaks, California on November 7, 2018.

Alaina Housley

Blake Dingman

Cody Coffman

Daniel Manrique

Jake Dunham

Justin Meek

Kristina Morisette

Mark Meza

Noel Sparks

Sgt. Ron Helus

Sean Adler

Telemachus Orfanos

Information about sexual violence
According to RAINN (Rape, Abuse & Incest National Network),
every 73 seconds, an American is sexually assaulted. And every 9
minutes, that victim is a child. Meanwhile, only 5 out of every
1,000 perpetrators will end up in prison.

If you are a victim of sexual violence RAINN operates the
National Sexual Assault Hotline at 800-656-HOPE or online at
https://hotline.rainn.org/online. If you need assistance, please
reach out to them.

Information about the history of lynching in America
To learn more about the form of terrorism known as lynching and
its lasting impacts in the United States, please visit the Equal
Justice Initiative's website at https://lynchinginamerica.eji.org/
explore. You can also read their report, Lynching in America,
which "documents more than 4400 racial terror lynchings in
the United States during the period between Reconstruction and
World War II." The report is available at https://eji.org/wp-
content/uploads/2020/09/lynching-in-america-3d-ed-091620.pdf.

Acknowledgements

My heart was full upon completing this collection. To have enough support, love, and encouragement to finish Grace Reflected and bring it into the world in the midst of a pandemic was a gift beyond measure. This collection would not exist without my Beloved, Bill, who is a constant source of grace in my life. My daughters are also gifts of grace that I'm grateful for every day.

The grief found in this book would not be as deep without the love that preceded the losses. Several poems in chapter five would not have been written if not for the love and friendship I felt for Will Carroll, Bruce Day, Marci Moore, Nora Wilson, William Brooks, Sr., and Rick Conte.

Mary Anne "Em" Radmacher has been a beacon, an inspiration, a source of guidance, and a source of delight in my life. Her many gifts helped me get to this moment of birth! My partners in Em's Mind Hive groups, Jean Martell, Jeanette Richardson Herring, Heather Ann Mack, Ann Bell, Marci Moore, Susan Paul Johnson, Karen C. L. Anderson, Dr. Kymn Harvin, Dr. Martina McGowan, Candace Doby, Liz Amaya-Fernandez, and Muse Sawyer all provided feedback, insights, and moral support along the way.

I have had many friends, acquaintances, and strangers who have provided opportunities for me to deepen my understanding of the legacy and costs of racism and enslavement in the United States. Among my teachers and partners on that path are Gaye Adegbalola, the late Dr. James Farmer, Eunice Hagler, Bill Brooks, Ainsley Brown, Kimbra Staten, Jesse Johnson, John Bernard, James Allen, and Rev. Doug McCusker. My learning around this critical issue is an ongoing process.

Lynda Allen is first and foremost a listener. All of her work whether writing, art, creating animal wisdom journals, or leading meditation begins with deep listening. Lynda listens to her own inner knowing and wisdom, the natural world, and the still small voice of the Divine in the silence. She listens. Then she creates.

In all of her creations she strives to inspire others to open their hearts and embrace their journey, both the dark and the light, with gentleness, love, and joy.

www.lyndaallen.net

CPSIA information can be obtained
at www.ICGtesting.com
Printed in the USA
BVHW031140050921
616108BV00008B/517